FONDUE COOKERY
ALISON BURT

First published by
Paul Hamlyn Pty Ltd. 1970
© Paul Hamlyn Pty 1970
This edition published
by the Hamlyn Publishing
Group Limited 1971
Astronaut House,
Feltham, Middlesex, England
Fifth impression 1974
ISBN 0 600 33465 1
Printed in the
Canary Islands (Spain)

Litografía A. Romero, S. A. - D. L. TF. 43 - 74

FONDUE COOKERY

ALISON BURT

HAMLYN
LONDON
SYDNEY
NEW YORK
TORONTO

PREFACE

During recent years you may have noticed the very attractive and practical kitchen pots and pans that have come on to the market. A far cry from the old style pans, this new equipment is made of heatproof pottery, stainless steel, attractively patterned enamel or beautiful copper—the choice is yours. Although some of the pans are made in this country, many are imported and bring with them some of the national characteristics of the country they came from. This is what has happened when fondue pots have been imported from France and Switzerland. A craze has started for table-top cookery. However, although many people enthusiastically buy fondue pots and chafing dishes, either for themselves or as presents, they find there is a scarcity of recipes and are very limited in the use of their new equipment.

In this book you will find a wide variety of recipes for using many types of table-top cooking equipment, fondue pots in particular.

CONTENTS

INTRODUCTION

What is a fondue? To different people it means different things. Most people know a fondue as the national dish of Switzerland, the Swiss Cheese Fondue. However if you look up 'fondue' in Larousse Gastronomique, the dictionary of food and cooking, you will find that a fondue can be a vegetable preparation that is cooked in butter or oil for a long time until it is reduced to a pulp. Yet another interpretation of a fondue is given by an 18th century gastronome, Brillat-Savarin, whose recipe for fondue is really scrambled eggs with cheese! All these types of fondue have one thing in common, they all involve the melting or blending of ingredients. This is how they originally came by their name; the French word "fondre' means to melt or blend.

As I mentioned before however, a fondue is recognised today as being the Cheese Fondue which is cooked in many homes around the world in a specially designed 'fondue pot', the cooking being done in front of the guests and everyone serving themselves from the communal fondue pot. Dessert fondues are also made by melting and so are true fondues but it has also become usage to call other dishes, that are cooked in a similar fashion, fondues. This is well illustrated in the section on Bourguignonne Fondues.

Conversion notes

American measurements have been used throughout this book. These are given in standard cups and spoons. Their capacity is as follows:

3 teaspoons = 1 tablespoon = ½ fluid ounce
2 tablespoons = 1 fluid ounce
4 tablespoons = ¼ cup = 2 fluid ounces
16 tablespoons = 1 cup = 8 fluid ounces
2 cups = 1 pint = 16 fluid ounces

Please note that: 1 American pint = 16 fluid ounces
                      1 British/Imperial pint = 20 fluid ounces
The American ½-pint measuring cup is therefore equal to ⅖ of a British pint.

Spoon and cup measures are always LEVEL. The American standard tablespoon (14·2 millilitres) is smaller than the British Standard (B.S.I.) tablespoon (17·7 millilitres). The following table gives equivalents using LEVEL standard spoons.

American	Imperial
1 teaspoon	1 teaspoon
1 tablespoon	1 tablespoon
2 tablespoons	1½ tablespoons
3 tablespoons	2 tablespoons
4 tablespoons	3 tablespoons

To convert American cup measurements into Imperial and metric measures please use the following table:

SOLID MEASURES

American	Imperial	Metric
2 cups butter	1 pound	450 grammes
4 cups flour	1 pound	450 grammes
¼ cup flour	1 ounce	28 grammes
2 cups crystal sugar	1 pound granulated sugar	450 grammes
2¼ cups castor sugar	1 pound	450 grammes
4 cups sifted icing sugar	1 pound	450 grammes
2½ cups soft brown sugar	1 pound	450 grammes
3 cups coarsely grated Swiss cheese	1 pound	450 grammes
4 cups finely grated Parmesan cheese	1 pound	450 grammes
4 cups grated Cheddar cheese	1 pound	450 grammes
8 cups soft breadcrumbs	1 pound	450 grammes
6 cups finely shredded cabbage	1 pound	450 grammes
1½ cups honey	1 pound	450 grammes
4 cups finely chopped almonds	1 pound	450 grammes

LIQUID MEASURES

American	Imperial	Metric
2 cups	16 fluid ounces	½ litre
1 cup	8 fluid ounces	¼ litre
1 tablespoon	½ fluid ounce	14·2 millilitres
3 tablespoons	2 tablespoons	42·6 millilitres
1 teaspoon	1 teaspoon	5·0 millilitres

CHEESE

A cheese fondue is a meal in itself.

The Swiss cheese fondue from which all the other fondues are derived is the traditional Neuchâtel Fondue and in the different cantons of Switzerland there are variations on this recipe. Fondues originally came into existence because of the geography and climate of Switzerland. In winter, when the mountains were covered with snow, the villages were cut off from the main towns. So fresh food was scarce and each village was forced to rely on its own resources. The locally made or produced foods—home baked bread, wine and cheese— were the main diet. As winter wore on the cheese became dryer and more and more unpalatable and so fondues were created in order to make the cheese more digestible—the melting of this dry, hard cheese in wine makes a most delicious meal. Many of you will already have experienced eating fondues in this very same atmosphere of a snowy mountain village, as it is traditional in skiing country to finish the day with a hot creamy cheese fondue.

Fondues are cooked and served in one communal pot. This again is a legacy from the Switzerland of long ago when the peasants were very poor and even cooking and eating utensils were scarce. Today we still use just one cooking pot and each person is given one fork to eat with—the style may have changed but the principle is still the same. The traditional fondue pot is made of earthenware, wide and shallow. It is called a 'caquelon' in Switzerland.

FONDUE PARTIES

It has become popular to hold fondue parties. The parties are usually quite intimate—only four or six people —and are terrific fun. All the preparation you have to do before your guests arrive is to set the dining table with a gay cloth, place the fondue pot and burner in the centre and a long fondue fork and plate for each guest.

INGREDIENTS FOR MAKING NEUCHATEL FONDUE

Set out on a tray the ingredients to make up the fondue, a cut clove of garlic, the opened bottle of dry white wine, coarsely grated cheese, the kirsch or brandy blended with cornflour, any flavourings and a loaf of crusty French bread on a bread board. The only cooking utensils needed are a balloon whisk or a wooden spoon and a knife to cut the bread.

Making the fondue is all part of the enjoyment and the guests should be encouraged to help. When the fondue has been prepared and is ready to eat, everyone sits around the table and then, in turn, each person spears a cube of bread on his fondue fork and swirls it in the fondue, in a figure-of-eight motion, until coated in cheese. He then eats it and the next person repeats the process. If each guest stirs the fondue when he dips in his bread, it will stay creamy until the end. It might be imagined that one could become very tipsy eating a fondue but this is not so because the alchohol evaporates off very quickly when the wine is heated. It is permitted to serve wine, the same as that used in the fondue, while eating although traditionally the only drink that is served is a small glass of kirsch or brandy half way through the meal. This is known as the 'coup de milieu'.

Although a fondue is sufficiently filling as a meal on its own, it can also be served as part of a meal. In Switzerland it is frequently preceded by dried meat, beef, for instance or partly-cooked ham, carved paper thin and served with a selection of pickled vegetables—gherkins, onion and cucumber. For a dessert—fruit salad, cherries 'a la kirsch' or in a tart.

I know that whichever way you serve your fondue, either by itself or as part of a meal, you will have great fun. To add to the enjoyment of the party, traditionally there are forfeits that are given when the guests drop a piece of bread into the fondue. The mildest forfeit is that one misses a turn in dipping but it is much more fun with the following forfeits: If a man drops his bread in the fondue he must either buy the next bottle of wine or else undertake to hold the next fondue party. If a lady drops her bread in the fondue, she must kiss all the men at the table!

A fondue party is essentially a friendly gathering. The delightfully relaxed atmosphere creates a general feeling of well-being and a fondue is so easy to make!

POINTS FOR MAKING A PERFECT FONDUE

An earthenware caquelon is definitely the best pot to use but cast iron fondue pots are quite satisfactory. Copper and stainless steel pots may be used but do take care—cheese burns very easily especially in a thin metal pot. The pot sits on a spirit burner and this must be very easily regulated.

Use cheese that is well matured.

Grate cheese very coarsely.

Use a dry white wine, e.g. riesling, chablis, hock. If you are in doubt as to whether the wine is dry enough, add a teaspoon of lemon juice. You will find this is recommended anyhow in some recipes. The acidity helps to melt the cheese.

Warm wine slightly before adding cheese.

Stir continuously until cheese is melted.

Stir in a figure-of-eight motion. This helps to blend the cheese into the wine.

Always keep the flame low. The cooking should be a slow gradual process for best results.

If the fondue curdles, add a few drops of lemon juice, heat and stir vigorously.

When the fondue is made you may consider that it is too thin; add more grated cheese or a little more corn-flour blended with warmed wine. If you think it is too thick add a little more warmed wine. The dryness of the cheese used can vary the consistency of the fondue.

Use French bread that is one day old. This is important, as it should not crumble when dipped into the fondue. Cut into 1-inch cubes and leave the crust on as this makes it easier to spear on the fondue fork. As a variation, toasted bread cubes or cubes of cold cooked potato can be served.

Bring fondue to simmering and allow to bubble slowly before and during the meal. Do not allow to boil. Stir frequently.

Serve white wine, the same as that used in the fondue, while the fondue is being prepared. Serve it at room temperature not chilled.

FONDUE NEUCHÂTEL
Traditional

SERVES 4

1 clove garlic
1 1/2 cups dry white wine
1 teaspoon lemon juice
2 cups (10 oz.) grated emmenthal cheese
2 cups (10 oz.) grated gruyère cheese
1 tablespoon cornflour
3 tablespoons kirsch
white pepper, grated nutmeg and paprika pepper
to taste
French bread, for serving

Rub the inside of fondue pot with a clove of garlic.
Heat the wine with the lemon juice carefully.
Add the cheese gradually stirring continuously in a
figure-of-eight motion.
When mixture is bubbling, add the kirsch and cornflour,
blended together.
Cook 2-3 minutes, season to taste.
Serve with French bread cut into 1-inch cubes.
Note: This is the traditional Swiss Fondue and forms the
base for other Fondues which are made in other parts of
Switzerland.
However, it is delicious in itself and I would advise you to
try it before experimenting with the variations.

CURRY FONDUE

SERVES 4

1 quantity Neuchâtel Fondue
2 tablespoons curry powder or to taste
French bread, for serving
mango chutney, drained, for serving

While preparing Neuchâtel Fondue, blend the curry
powder into the cornflour and kirsch mixture.
Serve with French bread cut into 1-inch cubes and spear
a piece of mango chutney on the fork behind the bread.

RICH FONDUE

SERVES 4

1 quantity Neuchâtel Fondue
pickled sweetcorn (cornichons), black and stuffed
olives, ham, thinly sliced salami, diced eggplant and
champignon sautéed lightly in butter, gherkins,
cooked prawns, apple, cooked sliced carrot,
cauliflower sprigs and a variety of breads, e.g. rye,
soya, French and crisply fried cubes of white bread,
for serving

Prepare Neuchâtel Fondue. Serve with any of the above
suggestions, cut into bite sized pieces. A piece of bread
should be speared on the fondue fork with one of the other
foods, for dipping.
Note: This is an ideal fondue for a big party. Leave all
the prepared ingredients on a large table to one side and
guests can come and help themselves as they please.
Make sure the fondue is kept well stirred to prevent burning.

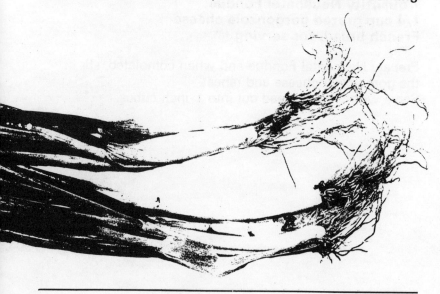

FARMER'S FONDUE

SERVES 4

1 quantity Neuchâtel Fondue
hot cooked potatoes, peeled and cut into 1/2-inch
cubes, 1/2-inch slices of frankfurter or vienna
sausage, large cocktail onions and gherkins for
serving

Prepare Neuchâtel Fondue. Serve with the above
suggestions.

GORGONZOLA FONDUE

SERVES 4

1 quantity Neuchâtel Fondue
1/4 cup grated gorgonzola cheese
French bread, for serving

Prepare Neuchâtel Fondue and when completed, stir in
the gorgonzola cheese and reheat.
Serve with French bread cut into 1-inch cubes.

HIS FONDUE

SERVES 4

1 quantity Neuchâtel Fondue
1 tablespoon dry mustard
pepper and cayenne pepper to taste
1 tablespoon snipped chives
French bread, for serving

While preparing Neuchâtel Fondue, blend the mustard,
pepper and cayenne pepper into the cornflour and kirsch
mixture. Sprinkle with chives before serving.
Serve with French bread cut into 1-inch cubes.

LANDLORD'S FONDUE

SERVES 4

1 quantity Neuchâtel Fondue
1 tablespoon finely chopped parsley
1 teaspoon each dried dill and tarragon
2 oz. bacon, diced and crisply fried
French bread, for serving

Mix all the ingredients together (except French bread)
as soon as Neuchâtel Fondue is prepared. Serve
immediately with French bread cut into 1-inch cubes.

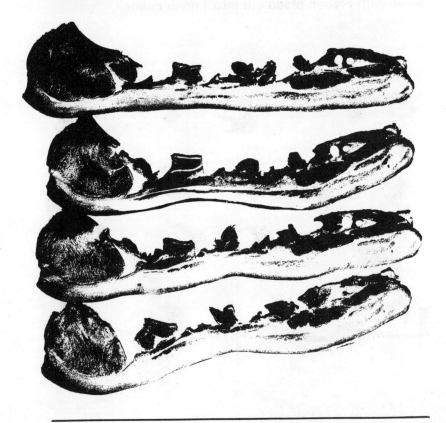

LUCERNE FONDUE

SERVES 6

1/2 cup white breadcrumbs
1 small onion, finely chopped
2 tablespoons chopped parsley
4 oz. minced beef (topside)
4 oz. minced pork
1 egg
salt and pepper
1/2 teaspoon marjoram
extra breadcrumbs
oil for frying
1 quantity Neuchâtel Fondue
bouquet garni
French bread, for serving

Mix breadcrumbs, onion, parsley, meats, egg, salt and pepper and majoram. Beat well. Form mixture into very small balls, roll in extra breadcrumbs and fry in oil until brown and crisped.
Prepare Neuchatel Fondue and add bouquet garni.
Serve with French bread cut into 1-inch cubes. Either meatballs or bread may be used for dipping into the fondue.

MEDITERRANEAN FONDUE

SERVES 4

1 quantity Neuchâtel Fondue
6 stuffed olives, thinly sliced
3 anchovies, chopped
1 clove garlic, crushed
French bread, for serving

Mix all ingredients together (except French bread) as soon as Neuchâtel Fondue is prepared and immediately before serving.
Serve with French bread cut into 1-inch cubes.

ROSÉ FONDUE

SERVES 4

Make and serve Fondue Neuchâtel as described on page11 only substitute rosé wine for white wine.

This Fondue was discovered in a chalet in the mountains when a group of skiers were stranded overnight. In the absence of white wine a dry rosé was substituted when making the Fondue for the evening meal. It gave the Fondue an unusual colour and such a deliciously different flavour that it has since been made very very often and is quite well known.

FONDUE SOUBISE

(Onion Fondue)

SERVES 4

2 onions
1 quantity Neuchâtel Fondue
cayenne pepper to taste
French bread, for serving

Grate onions and place in a small saucepan with the
juices. Cook over a low heat until soft and very tender.
Stir cooked onion into prepared Neuchâtel Fondue with
the cayenne pepper.
Serve with French bread cut into 1-inch cubes.

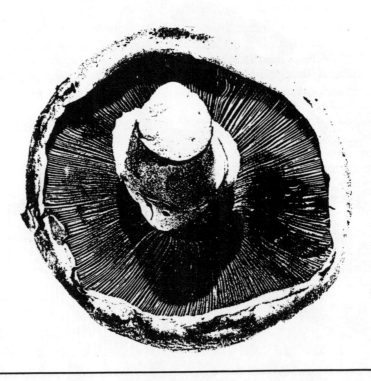

AVOCADO FONDUE

SERVES 4-6

4 oz. butter
1 medium sized onion, finely chopped
1/2 cup (2 oz.) flour
1 cup milk
1/2 cup cream
salt and pepper
4 tablespoons lemon juice
1 cup avocado, well mashed
1/2 cup (2 oz.) parmesan cheese
brandy to taste
1 lb. cooked shrimps, for serving
thin slices brown bread and butter

Melt the butter in fondue pot, add the onion and sauté
gently until soft. Stir in flour and cook for 2-3 minutes.
Remove from heat, add milk, cream, salt, pepper, lemon
juice and avocado. Stir well, cook for 5 minutes stirring
constantly, do not allow to boil. Add cheese, stir until
melted. Blend in brandy.
Use peeled shrimps for dipping into the Avocado Fondue.
Serve brown bread and butter separately.

BEER FONDUE

SERVES 3-4

1 cup beer
2 cups (8 oz.) cheddar cheese, grated
1 clove garlic, crushed
1 oz. butter
1/2 teaspoon dry mustard
2 tablespoons cornflour
little extra beer
French bread, for serving

Place beer, cheese and garlic in fondue pot. Cook over a low heat, stirring constantly, until cheese has melted. Stir in butter. Blend mustard, cornflour with a little extra beer. Add to fondue, stir until thickened.
Serve with French bread cut into 1-inch cubes

FONDUE DE BERNE

SERVES 4-6

1 clove garlic
1 cup dry white wine
4 cups (1 lb. 4 oz.) emmenthal cheese coarsely grated
4 egg yolks
5 tablespoons cream
grated nutmeg and paprika pepper to taste
French bread, for serving

Rub inside of fondue pot with cut clove garlic. Heat wine carefully, do not boil. Add cheese and stir until smooth. Beat egg yolks with cream and add to fondue pot. Blend, add seasoning and stir until mixture is thick and creamy. Serve with French bread, cut into 1-inch cubes.

BLUE RIBBON FONDUE

SERVES 3-4

1 clove garlic
1 cup dry white wine
3 cups (1 lb.) gruyère cheese, coarsely grated
1 teaspoon arrowroot
1 tablespoon kirsch
1/2 oz. butter
French bread, for serving

Rub inside of fondue pot with cut clove garlic. Mix together wine and cheese and place in pot over a medium heat; stir continually until thick. Blend the arrowroot with the kirsch, stir into the mixture to bind and add the butter. Serve with French bread cut into 1-inch cubes.

PEASANT FONDUE

SERVES 4-6

2 cups tomato purée
1 clove garlic, crushed
4 cups (1 lb. 4 oz.) Swiss cheese, grated
2 tablespoons cream
1 tablespoon cornflour
pepper
oregano
French bread and cabonossi, for serving

Heat tomato purée in fondue pot with garlic. Add cheese and stir until melted. Blend cream with cornflour and add to tomato mixture. Stir until thickened, season with pepper and oregano.
Serve with French bread and cabonossi cut into 1-inch pieces.

SALMON FONDUE

SERVES 4-6

8 oz. butter
4 onions, chopped
4 cups (1 lb.) cheddar cheese, diced
3/4 cup tomato sauce
4 tablespoons worcestershire sauce
1/4 cup sherry
salt and pepper
2 cups canned salmon, drained and flaked
French bread, for serving

Melt butter, sauté onions gently until soft. Add cheese, sauce, worcestershire sauce, sherry and seasonings. Stir constantly until smooth. Add salmon and blend well.
Serve with French bread cut into 1-inch cubes.

FONDUE FLAMBÉ

SERVES 3-4

1/2 bottle dry white wine
8 oz. Swiss cheese, diced
1/2 cup (2 oz.) flour
1 cup kirsch
French bread, for serving

Place 1/2 pint of the wine in fondue pot, add cheese and stir over a low heat until cheese is melted and fondue begins to bubble. Add kirsch, quickly set alight. Serve while flame is still burning.
Cut French bread into long fingers for serving.

BLUSHING FONDUE

SERVES 3-4

1 1/2 cups (6 oz.) cheshire cheese, grated
1/2 cup (2 oz.) blue cheese, grated
1/2 cup condensed tomato soup
1 teaspoon worcestershire sauce
3 tablespoons sherry
French bread and Continental sausage, for serving

Mix together in fondue pot, cheeses, tomato soup and worcestershire sauce. Heat gently, stirring constantly, until cheese is melted and mixture is creamy. Stir in the sherry. Serve with French bread and Continental sausage cut into 1-inch cubes.

OYSTER CHEESE FONDUE

SERVES 3-4

1 clove garlic
1 can condensed oyster soup
1/2 cup milk
1 3/4 cups (8 oz.) Swiss cheese, grated
1/4 teaspoon dry mustard
pepper to taste
French bread, for serving

Rub the inside of fondue pot with cut clove of garlic. Place soup in pot, add milk and whisk until smooth. Add cheese, stir over a low heat until cheese melts. Season. Serve with French bread cut into 1-inch cubes.

CIDER FONDUE

SERVES 4-6

1 clove garlic
1 1/2 cups dry cider
2 cups (8 oz.) cheddar cheese, grated
1 3/4 cups (8 oz.) Swiss cheese, grated
4 teaspoons cornflour
1/2 teaspoon dry mustard
pepper
2 tablespoons calvados
French bread, for serving

Rub inside of fondue pot with cut clove garlic. Put
1 1/4 cups cider in pot and place over a low heat until
warm. Add cheeses and stir until melted. Blend remaining
1/4 cup cider with cornflour, mustard and pepper to taste.
Add to fondue pot and stir until fondue is bubbling and
thickened. Stir in calvados.
Serve with French bread cut into 1-inch cubes.

HALF AND HALF FONDUE

SERVES 4-6

1 clove garlic
1 cup dry white wine
1 teaspoon lemon juice
2 cups (10 oz.) gruyère cheese, grated
2 cups (10 oz.) taffel cheese,
grated
2 tablespoons cornflour
1/4 cup brandy
French bread, for serving

Rub inside of fondue pot with cut clove garlic. Put wine and lemon juice in pot over low heat until warmed. Add cheeses and stir until melted. Blend cornflour and brandy together and add to fondue pot, stir until fondue is bubbling and blended.
Serve with French bread cut into 1-inch cubes.
Note: If taffel cheese is not available, substitute edam.

FONDUE CHERIE

SERVES 4-6

1 clove garlic
2 cups riesling
3 cups (1 lb.) grated Swiss cheese
4 tablespoons flour
1/2 teaspoon salt
pinch of pepper
3 tablespoons brandy
French bread, for serving

Rub fondue pot and spoon with cut clove of garlic.
Heat wine carefully, do not boil. Add cheese to wine,
stir until melted and bubbly. Add seasoning and stir in
brandy.
Serve with French bread cut into 1-inch cubes.

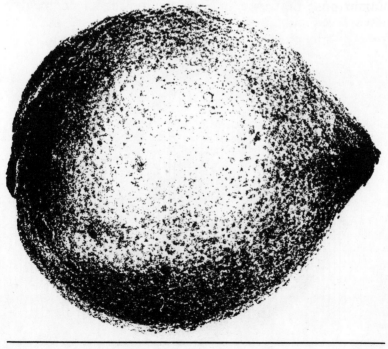

LOBSTER FONDUE

SERVES 4-6

1 oz. butter
2 oz. mushrooms, roughly chopped
1 lb. lobster meat, cubed
4 tablespoons sherry
salt, cayenne pepper, paprika pepper
3 egg yolks
1 cup cream
French bread, for serving

Melt butter in fondue pot, fry mushrooms gently until
cooked. Add the cubed lobster, sherry and seasoning,
Beat egg yolks, then stir in cream. Blend this mixture with
the other ingredients. Stir until smooth.
Serve with French bread cut into 1-inch cubes.
Variations: Crab meat or tuna, can replace lobster meat.

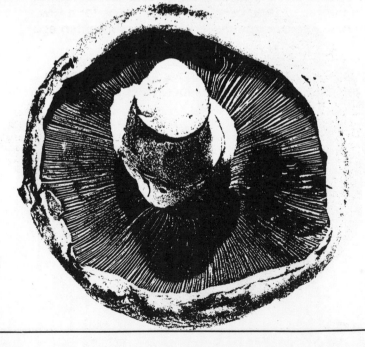

DEVILLED FONDUE

SERVES 3-4

8 oz. cheddar cheese, diced
1/2 oz. butter
1 tablespoon flour
1/3 cup milk
1 teaspoon worcestershire sauce
3/4 teaspoon horseradish relish
1/2 teaspoon salt
pepper to taste
1/2 teaspoon paprika pepper
1 egg, separated
2 tablespoons sherry
French bread, for serving

Melt butter and cheese in fondue pot over a very low heat.
Stir in flour and then warmed milk and seasoning, stir
until thickened. Add beaten egg yolk, cook for a few
minutes. Remove from heat. Fold in stiffly beaten egg
white and sherry.
Serve with French bread cut into 1-inch cubes.
Variation: 2 teaspoons anchovy sauce can replace
horseradish for a different flavour. Omit salt.

COTTAGE FONDUE

SERVES 4-6

1 clove garlic
2 oz. butter
1/2 cup (2 oz.) flour
1 1/2 cups milk
1 cup (4 oz.) grated pecorino cheese
1 cup cottage cheese
1/2 teaspoon salt
4 tablespoons sherry
French bread, for serving

Rub the inside of the fondue pot with cut clove of garlic. Melt butter, stir in flour and blend over a low heat for 2-3 minutes. Slowly add milk stirring constantly. Stir in cheeses and heat until mixture is thick and creamy. Add salt and sherry.
Serve with French bread cut into 1-inch cubes.

Fondue dishes shown on the following four colour pages are (in order):

SWISS BREAD 'ROSTI'

DEEP SOUTH FONDUE

CARAMEL FONDUE

RICH FONDUE

INNERSCHWEIZ FONDUE

SERVES 4

2 oz. butter
1/2 cup (2 oz.) flour
1 1/4 cups milk
salt
1 1/2 cups (7 oz.) gruyère cheese, grated
1/2 cup (2 oz.) blue cheese, finely grated
1/2 cup dry white wine
freshly ground white pepper
French bread, for serving

Melt butter in fondue pot, stir in flour and cook, stirring,
1-2 minutes. Remove from heat, add milk gradually,
stirring constantly. Bring to boil and cook until very thick.
Add salt to taste. Add gruyère cheese, stir until melted then
add blue cheese. Gradually stir in wine and bring to boil.
Season with pepper.
Serve with French bread cut into 1-inch cubes.

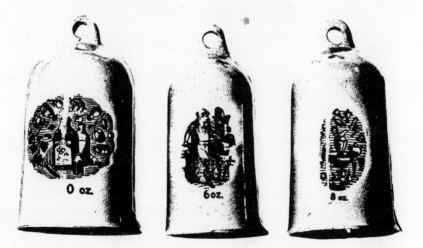

FONDUE JEUNESSE

SERVES 4-6

2 oz. butter
3 tablespoons flour
1 1/2 cups dry white wine, heated
3 egg yolks
1 cup (5 oz.) freshly grated Swiss cheese
1 tablespoon cream
nutmeg, salt and cayenne pepper to taste
French bread, for serving

Melt butter, add flour, blend and cook for 2-3 minutes.
Add heated wine slowly, stirring constantly. When mixture
is thickened, add cheese and stir until smooth. Beat egg
yolks and cream together and add to the mixture. Blend
well then stir in the seasonings.
Serve with French bread cut into 1-inch cubes.

FONDUE MARSEILLAISE

SERVES 4-6

1 cup (5 oz.) grated Swiss cheese
6 tablespoons flour
2 cups milk
1/2 teaspoon cayenne pepper
1 tablespoon worcestershire sauce
1/2 teaspoon dry mustard
1 teaspoon salt
peeled shrimps, for serving

Mix cheese with flour and place in fondue pot with milk and seasoning. Stir over medium heat until smooth and creamy.
Use shrimps for dipping into the Fondue Marseillaise.

MUSHROOM FONDUE

SERVES 6

2 oz. butter
3/4 lb. mushrooms, finely sliced
1 medium sized onion, peeled and chopped
3 tablespoons flour
1 cup milk
3/4 cup (3 oz.) cheddar cheese, grated
1/2 cup cream
salt and pepper
2 tablespoons chopped parsley
Curried Bread Cubes, for serving

Melt butter in fondue pot and gently fry mushrooms and onion for 10 minutes. Sprinkle in flour and add milk. Bring to the boil, stirring, until thickened. Cook for 2 minutes. Add cheese, stir over a low heat until melted. Stir in cream, add seasonings to taste. Sprinkle with chopped parsley.

Curried Bread Cubes:
1 small white unsliced loaf
2 oz. butter
2 tablespoons oil
4 teaspoons curry powder

Remove crusts from loaf and cut into 3/4-inch cubes. Heat butter and oil together in frying pan, stir in curry powder. Fry bread cubes until golden brown and crisp. Drain well before serving.

SIMPLE CHEDDAR FONDUE

SERVES 4-6

1 clove garlic
4 cups (1 lb.) cheddar cheese, grated
1/2 cup milk
1 teaspoon dry mustard
salt and pepper to taste
1 egg yolk
French bread and tart apples, for serving.

Rub the inside of the fondue pot with cut clove of garlic.
Melt the cheese in the fondue pot over a very low heat.
Stir in milk and seasonings. Add egg yolk and reheat
fondue, stirring constantly, until slightly thickened and
creamy.
Serve with French bread cut into 1-inch cubes and tart
apples, peeled, cored and cut into bite sized pieces.
Spear a cube of bread and a piece of apple on fondue fork
for dipping.

PETER'S FONDUE

SERVES 3-4

1 onion, finely chopped
4 oz. butter
1/2 cup (2 oz.) plain flour
1 cup milk
1/2 cup puréed chicken livers
1/2 cup cream
1/2 cup tomato paste
2 tablespoons worcestershire sauce
1 teaspoon cayenne pepper
salt to taste
1/2 cup (2 oz.) parmesan cheese
1/4 cup cognac
French bread, for serving

Melt butter, sauté onion gently until soft. Stir in flour and cook for 2-3 minutes. Add milk, puréed chicken livers, cream, tomato paste, worcestershire sauce, cayenne pepper and salt. Cover and cook gently, stirring occasionally for 10 minutes. Remove from heat and add cheese, stir until melted. Blend in cognac.
Serve with French bread cut into 1-inch cubes.

FONDUE PRINCESS

SERVES 4-6

2 oz. mushroom caps
2 cups champagne
3 cups (1 lb.) grated Swiss cheese
4 tablespoons flour
2 egg yolks
salt and pepper to taste
French bread, for serving

Cook mushroom caps in boiling water to cover, for 5 minutes. Drain, reserving 1/4 cup of liquor, and slice thinly.

Heat champagne slowly in fondue pot, do not boil. Stir in cheese and flour, mixed together and blend until smooth. Beat the egg yolks with the reserved mushroom liquor and add with the sliced mushrooms. Season to taste and reheat without boiling.

Serve with French bread cut into 1-inch cubes.

TOMATO FONDUE

SERVES 3-4

1 onion, sliced
1 1/2 oz. butter
1 clove garlic, crushed
1/4 teaspoon dried thyme
2 medium sized tomatoes, skinned and chopped
salt and pepper
3 tablespoons grated parmesan cheese
frankfurter sausages

Fry onion gently in fondue pot in melted butter, until
soft. Add garlic, thyme, tomatoes and seasoning. Stir to
combine, then cover and simmer for 30 minutes. Add
parsley and cheese, stir until thick and smooth.
Cook frankfurters in boiling water for 2 minutes and cut
into 1-inch sections. Use the frankfurter sections for
dipping into the tomato fondue.

THREE CHEESE FONDUE

SERVES 4

6 eggs, beaten
4 oz. butter
1 cup (5 oz.) grated gruyère cheese
1 cup (4 oz.) grated cheddar cheese
1/2 cup (2 oz.) freshly grated parmesan cheese
1/2 cup dry white wine or cream
salt and pepper
toast or French bread, for serving

Beat eggs well with a fork. Pour into a fondue pot and set over a very low heat. When eggs are beginning to set, add the butter in small pieces and, when melted, add the cheese and wine or cream. Season and stir until thickened and creamy.
Serve with toast or French bread, cut into 1-inch cubes.

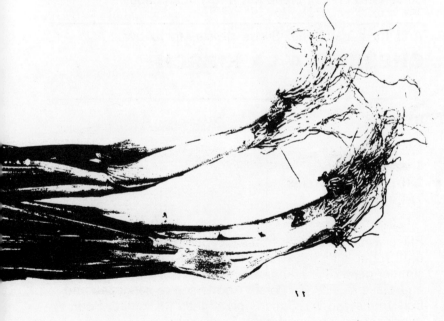

SWISS FONDUE

SERVES 3-4

1 clove garlic
2 1/2 cups dry white wine
3 cups (1 lb.) Swiss cheese, grated
pepper
2 oz. cornflour
1/2 cup kirsch
French bread, for serving

Rub the inside of the fondue pot with cut clove of garlic.
Add the wine to the pot, warm slightly then stir in cheese.
Cook over a low heat, stirring constantly, until cheese
is melted and mixture begins to bubble. Add pepper to
taste. Blend cornflour with kirsch and add. Stir until
fondue has thickened.
Serve with French bread cut into 1-inch cubes.

And for a traditional Swiss dessert to follow.....

CHERRIES À LA KIRSCH

SERVES 4

1/2 cup water
4 oz. sugar
1 lb. black cherries
1/4 cup kirsch

Place water and sugar in a saucepan. Heat, stirring,
until sugar is dissolved and syrup boils. Add cherries and
simmer gently for 10 minutes. Remove cherries carefully
and place in a serving dish. Add kirsch to saucepan and
boil until syrup is reduced and slightly thickened. Pour
over cherries, cool and chill. Serve cold.

or . . . . . .

CHERRY TART

SERVES   6
TIME   25 minutes
TEMPERATURE   400-425°F

Pastry:
1 1/2 cups (6 oz.) plain flour
1/2 teaspoon salt
1 1/2 oz. butter
1 1/2 oz. lard
3 tablespoons water

1 lb. cherries, pitted
6 oz. castor sugar
2 tablespoons red currant jelly

To make pastry: Sift flour and salt into a bowl. Rub in
butter and lard with your fingertips until mixture resembles
fine breadcrumbs. Add the water gradually and mix, with
a round bladed knife, to a firm dough. Knead lightly.
Cover and chill in refrigerator for 30 minutes.
Roll out pastry and line an 8-inch tart plate. Cover
pastry with cherries and sprinkle castor sugar over. Bake
in a hot oven for 25 minutes. About 5 minutes before tart
is ready, spread the red currant jelly over the cherries.
Allow to cool then chill and serve cold.

DESSERT

These delicious fondues are the most wonderful way to finish a meal. Their origin is vague but a New York restaurant is said to be the first place ever to serve a chocolate fondue. Dessert fondues are rapidly becoming more and more popular now and the variations are endless, limited only by your own imagination. The recipes given in this book are only basic ones to which you can add your own choice of flavourings or other ingredients to personalise the fondue.

These fondues are very quickly made if the ingredients are all at hand and are brought to the table when just below boiling point. A spirit burner is needed to keep the fondue hot. The best type of pot in which to make and serve the fondue is made of heatproof earthenware. It should be shallow and wide, metal pots can be used but cream is very delicate and the fondue may burn unless great care is taken.

The most interesting part of a dessert fondue is the variety of foods that can be used for dipping. The hostess supplies bowls full of fresh fruit; apricots, peaches, strawberries, paw paw and so on, all cut into bite sized pieces. Other suggestions are sponge fingers, cubes of butter cake, marshmallows and macaroons. Each guest is given a plate and a long fondue fork and serves himself, eating in the same manner as for a cheese fondue.

This dessert is most popular with children—which goes without saying. It is also the ideal dish to serve when friends come to dinner, to round off a perfect meal.

HONEY ALMOND FONDUE

SERVES 4

8 oz, milk chocolate
1/2 cup cream
1/4 cup honey
1/2 cup finely chopped almonds
fresh fruit, cake and biscuits, for serving

Grate chocolate, place in fondue pot with cream and
honey. Heat gently, stirring, until smooth and melted.
Stir in almonds.
Serve with fresh fruit, cake and biscuits (see introduction).

MILK CHOCOLATE FONDUE

SERVES 4

8 oz. milk chocolate
1/2 cup cream
2 tablespoons kirsch
fresh fruit, cake and biscuits, for serving

Grate chocolate and put into fondue pot with cream.
Stir well and heat gently, stirring until chocolate is melted.
Add kirsch and blend.
Serve with fresh fruit, cake and biscuits (see introduction).

Variations: Omit kirsch and substitute with 1-2
tablespoons of one of the following liqueurs—tia maria,
crème de cacao or grand marnier. If the fondue is to be
served to children, omit kirsch and, if liked, add a few
drops peppermint, vanilla or orange essence.

CREAM FONDUE

SERVES 4-6

2 cups cream
1 cup icing sugar
vanilla, almond or peppermint
essence to taste
2 tablespoons cornflour
fresh fruit, cake and biscuits, for serving

Mix 1 1/2 cups cream with icing sugar in fondue pot.
Heat gently stirring until melted. Blend rest of cream with
cornflour, add to fondue pot and stir until thickened. Add
essence to taste.
Serve with fresh fruit, cake and biscuits (see introduction).

MOCHA FONDUE

SERVES 4

8 oz. milk chocolate
1 tablespoon instant coffee powder
3/4 cup cream
1 tablespoon tia maria, optional
fresh fruit, cake and biscuits, for serving

Grate chocolate and mix with coffee powder. Put cream
in fondue pot, add chocolate/coffee mixture and blend.
Heat gently, stirring until smooth and melted. Add tia
maria, if desired, and blend.
Serve with fresh fruit, cake and biscuits (see introduction).

FRUIT CREAM FONDUE

SERVES 4-6

1 cup cream
3/4 cup fruit purée (strawberry, raspberry,
black currant, cooked apricots or plums)
1/2 cup icing sugar
1 tablespoon cornflour
cake or biscuits, for serving

Blend all ingredients together in fondue pot. Heat, stirring,
until smooth and thickened.
Serve with cake or biscuits (see introduction).

CARAMEL FONDUE

SERVES 4-6

1/2 cup castor sugar
2 cups cream
2 tablespoons cornflour
fresh fruit, cake or biscuits, for serving

Place castor sugar in fondue pot. Heat very gently until
sugar is golden brown and liquid. Blend cream with
cornflour and add. Stir well until caramel has dissolved
and fondue has thickened.
Serve with fresh fruit, cake and biscuits (see introduction)

DEEP SOUTH FONDUE

SERVES 4

8 oz. dark chocolate
1/2 cup cream
1/4 teaspoon each ground cinnamon,
nutmeg and cloves
fresh fruit, cake and biscuits, for serving

Grate chocolate, place in fondue pot. Add cream and
spices, blend well. Heat gently, stirring until smooth
and blended.
Serve with fresh fruit, cake and biscuits (see introduction).
Variation: Omit spices and add 1 tablespoon grated
orange rind.

PRALINE FONDUE

SERVES 4-6

1/2 cup castor sugar
vanilla essence to taste
3/4 cup almonds, toasted
2 cups cream
2 tablespoons cornflour
fresh fruit, cake or biscuits for serving

Put castor sugar and vanilla into a small saucepan. Place
over a low heat and leave until sugar is liquid and golden
brown. Add almonds. Pour onto a lightly greased cake tin
and allow to become cold. Grind very finely (an electric
blender is ideal for this purpose).
Put cream into fondue pot, blend in cornflour and stir
until thickened. Stir in praline.
Serve with fresh fruit, cake and biscuits (see introduction).

BOURGUIGNONNE FONDUES

Bourguignonne Fondue is the name given to a range of fondues that are meat or fish cooked in oil or stock in a communal fondue pot at the table. However this name really only applies to the first recipe in this chapter which originated in the Burgundy district of France—the Beef Fondue.

With all these fondues the guests cook and serve their own food. Prior to the meal the hostess fills the fondue pot one-third to half full with oil or stock (according to the recipe). The pot is then heated until very hot, oil should be at a temperature of 375°F. (a $\frac{1}{4}$-inch dice of bread, when put in the oil, should brown in less than a minute), and stock should be boiling. These temperatures should be maintained throughout the cooking time so the fondue pot must be made of a heat retaining material. The best pots are made of cast iron but those made of stainless steel and copper are also very satisfactory. Around the fondue pot on the dining table are placed small bowls with the accompanying sauces and also any other dishes recommended for serving with the fondue. A fondue fork, a dinner fork and a fondue plate are set on the table for each person. Special fondue forks and plates are available but ordinary ones will do in an emergency. The main ingredients of the fondue are carefully prepared as given in the recipes and arranged on a large serving plate. This preparation can be done well in advance, the meat covered and stored in the refrigerator, but make sure that it is very dry before serving for cooking as moisture will cause oil to spit.

When all is ready, the fun begins. After selecting his choice of accompaniments, each person spears a piece of meat on his fondue fork. Remember that the fork should go right through the meat with about 1/4-inch showing on the other side, this allows the fork to touch the bottom of the pot, not the meat, and prevents sticking. The meat is immersed in the oil or stock until cooked. It is then transferred to the dinner fork, dipped in one of the sauces and eaten. You will find that each person will become his own expert cook, making sure his meat is done just as he likes it!!

The recipes for the sauces follow this chapter. You need not keep strictly to the sauces suggested in the fondue recipes, introduce those of your own choice to give the meal a personal touch. The dishes served with the fondue may also be varied to your personal taste, though those suggested compliment the meal and are the ideal.

BOURGUIGNONNE FONDUE

6-8 oz. fillet beef, per person
peanut oil for frying
1 bayleaf (optional)

Accompaniments
Garlic Sauce   (see recipe page 71)
Andalouse Sauce   (see recipe page 67)
Horseradish Sauce   (see recipe page 67)
Rémoulade Sauce   (see recipe page 79)
(Other sauces may be selected from those given in the
Sauce chapter)
mustard pickles
black olives
thinly sliced raw onion rings
salt and pepper

For serving
Tossed Green Salad
Tomatoes Vinaigrette
French bread

Remove all the sinews and fat from the meat and cut into
1-inch cubes.
Put enough oil into fondue pot to fill it 1/3 to 1/2 full.
Heat oil until very hot (375°F) on a sugar thermometer,
or until a dice of bread will brown in less than a minute,
then regulate fondue burner just to maintain the
temperature of the oil. Add bay leaf to oil if desired.
Guests select their own choice of accompaniments. Each
person then spears a cube of meat on his fondue fork
and places the meat in the hot oil. The meat only takes a
few moments to cook, the exact time will depend on the
taste of the individual. The meat is then seasoned with a
sauce and transferred to another fork for eating.

TOSSED GREEN SALAD

SERVES 4-6

1 large lettuce
1 cucumber, peeled and thinly sliced
4 shallots, sliced
1 green capsicum, sliced in rings
French Dressing

Wash lettuce well, drain and chill until crisp. Mix salad vegetables together and add enough French Dressing to moisten. Toss salad lightly.
Note: Other green salad vegetables such as endive, watercress and young spinach may be added to the above if liked.

FRENCH DRESSING
6 tablespoons oil
2 tablespoons white vinegar
1 teaspoon French mustard
1/2 teaspoon salt
1/2 teaspoon freshly ground pepper

Mix all ingredients together thoroughly. Place in a bowl and whisk vigorously with a fork or place in a screw-top jar and shake well. The finished dressing should be thick and creamy.
Note: Chopped herbs may be added if desired.

TOMATOES VINAIGRETTE

SERVES 4

4 tomatoes
French dressing (see recipe page 53)
1 teaspoon finely chopped capers
1 teaspoon finely chopped olives
1 tablespoon chopped parsley

Slice tomatoes thinly, arrange in serving dish. To
French dressing, add capers, olives and parsley and mix
well. Pour over tomatoes and allow to marinate for 30
minutes before serving.

GARLIC BREAD

SERVES	4-6
TIME	30 minutes
TEMPERATURE	400-425°F.

1 long French loaf
6 oz. butter
6 cloves garlic (or to taste)

Make cuts in the loaf at 1 to 1 1/2-inch intervals. Do not
cut right through, leave 1/4-inch of bread joining the
slices together at base. Crush garlic well, beat into butter.
Spread a generous amount of garlic butter between slices
of bread, using all the butter. Wrap in aluminium foil and
bake in a hot oven for 30 minutes or until hot and crisp.

AUSTRALIAN LAMB FONDUE

SERVES 4

6-8 oz. prime quality lamb,
cut from leg, per person
peanut oil for frying

Accompaniments
Curry Sauce   (see recipe page 73)
Mint Sauce   (see recipe page 74)
Onion Sauce   (see recipe page 69)
Cumberland Sauce   (see recipe page 72)
(Other sauces may be selected from those given in the
Sauce chapter)
apricot chutney or other fruit chutneys
salt and pepper

For serving
Pacific Coleslaw
Garlic Bread

Prepare, cook and serve as given in the recipe for
Bourguignonne Fondue substituting lamb for beef.

FONDUE SAUCISSON

SERVES 4

1 lb. variety Continental sausage
e.g. cabonossi, knackwurst, salami, etc.
8 oz. Swiss cheese
oil for frying

Accompaniments
Rémoulade Sauce   (see recipe page 79)
Tomato Sauce   (see recipe page 75)
Swedish Sauce   (see recipe page 65)
Cucumber Sauce   (see recipe page 68)

For serving
French mustard
Pickled onions
Salad Niçoise
French bread and butter

Prepare fondue pot, fill to 1/3 – 1/2 full with oil. Heat until very hot (375°F.) or until a dice of bread will brown in less than a minute, then regulate fondue burner just to maintain the temperature of the oil.
Guests spear a cube of cheese then a cube of sausage on a fondue fork. The cheese and sausage are then put in the hot oil just until the cheese begins to melt. They are then seasoned to taste and transferred to another fork for eating.

SALADE NIÇOISE

SERVES 4

1 lettuce
8 oz. cooked French beans
8 black olives, pitted
1/2 cup French Dressing (see recipe page 53)
4 tomatoes, quartered
8 fillets anchovy
little chopped chervil
little chopped tarragon

Wash and dry lettuce, put into refrigerator to crisp.
Cut the French beans into 1/2-inch pieces. Mix together
beans and olives and toss in French Dressing. Place on a
bed of lettuce and arrange tomatoes and anchovies on
top. Sprinkle with chopped herbs.

Accompaniments for Australian Lamb Fondue

PACIFIC COLESLAW

SERVES 4-6

3 cup finely shredded cabbage
1/4 cup diced celery
1/4 cup diced red capsicum
1/4 cup canned pineapple pieces, drained
1 orange, cut into sections
1/4 cup grapes, seeded and peeled
1/2 cup French Dressing (see recipe page 53)

Chill cabbage well. Add celery, capsicum, pineapple,
orange and grapes. Chill again until needed. Just before
serving pour French Dressing over salad and toss lightly.

ORIENTAL FIRE KETTLE DINNER
(Oriental Fondue)

6-8 oz. meat per person
mixture of the following:
paper thin slices beef fillet, veal kidney, veal
fillet, pork fillet, lambs' kidney and lambs' fry;
bite sized pieces of cooked chicken, green prawns
chicken stock
1/2-inch green ginger

Accompaniments
Sweet and Sour Sauce   (see recipe page 74)
Black Bean Sauce   (see recipe page 70)
Plum Sauce   (see recipe page 77)
Piquant Sauce   (see recipe page 78)
(Other sauces may be selected from those given in the
Sauce chapter)
toasted almonds or salted peanuts
salt and pepper

For Serving
Fried Rice
Mandarin Salad or a selection of crisp salad vegetables,
radishes, grated carrots, sliced bamboo shoot, water
chestnuts and spring onions arranged on a bed of
Chinese cabbage or lettuce
Sherry

Arrange the meat in overlapping circles attractively on
a large serving platter. Heat chicken stock until boiling
and pour into fire kettle, add green ginger. Make sure
stock is kept at boiling point throughout the cooking time.
Guests select their own choice of accompaniments. Each
person then spears a slice of meat on his fondue fork (or
picks it up with chopsticks) and places the meat in the
boiling stock. The meat must be very thin so that it only
takes about a minute to cook. The meat is then seasoned
with a sauce and transferred to another fork for eating.
When the meal has been completed, add sherry to taste

to the broth and serve it to each person in individual soup bowls. The broth is delicious having had the meats cooked in it and no further seasoning will be necessary. *Note:* Chinese Fire Kettles may be purchased at Chinese stores which sell kitchen equipment. However, a metal fondue pot may be used with equally satisfactory results.

Accompaniments for Oriental Fire Kettle Dinner

MANDARIN SALAD

SERVES 4-6

1 can mandarin orange sections
1 small can lychees in syrup
4-5 lettuce leaves (or Chinese cabbage, if available)
5 tablespoons salad oil
3 tablespoons vinegar
1 tablespoon toasted sesame seeds
1 teaspoon soy sauce
1 teaspoon sugar
1/4 teaspoon monosodium glutamate
1/2 teaspoon dry mustard
salt and pepper to taste
1 cup thin matchstick bamboo shoots
3 shallots, chopped
1/2 cup sliced water chestnuts

Drain syrup from oranges and lychees. Shred lettuce leaves coarsely, put into a bowl, cover and chill. Combine oil, vinegar, sesame seeds, soy sauce, sugar, monosodium glutamate, mustard, salt and pepper. Add bamboo shoots, shallots and water chestnuts. Marinate for 1 hour. Mix in the oranges, lychees and lettuce, toss lightly.

FRIED RICE

SERVES 4

oil
1 clove garlic
2 oz. blanched almonds, split in halves
1 egg, beaten
2 cups cold boiled rice
3 shallots, sliced thinly
4 oz. thin slices barbecued pork
salt to taste
pinch of monosodium glutamate
2 tablespoons soy sauce

Heat 2 tablespoons oil with the garlic clove. Remove garlic when browned and discard. Fry almonds gently until lightly browned. Drain. If necessary add a little more oil. Pour in egg and when half set, add rice and stir quickly so that grains become coated with egg. Add shallots, pork, salt and monosodium glutamate. Turn over and over steadily for a few minutes. Stir in almonds, sprinkle in the soy sauce and cook for 2 minutes.

FISH FONDUE

**6-8 oz. mixture raw white fish and
shellfish per person, cut into bite sized
pieces
peanut oil for frying**

Accompaniments
Mushroom Sauce   (see recipe page 80)
Thousand Island Sauce   (see recipe page 66)
Egg and Lemon Sauce   (see recipe page 66)
Tartare Sauce   (see recipe page 65)
(Other sauces may be selected from those given in
the Sauce chapter)
lemon wedges
salt and pepper

For Serving
Thin slices buttered brown bread

Wipe fish, dry well and season. Cook and serve as for
Bourguignonne Fondue, substituting fish for beef.
Note: If using scallops, remove coral before frying
otherwise the oil will spit badly.

SAUCES

BASIC MAYONNAISE

2 egg yolks
1/2 teaspoon salt
1/2 teaspoon dry mustard
1/4 teaspoon castor sugar
3 tablespoons fresh lemon juice (strained)
1 1/4 cups olive oil
1 tablespoon wine vinegar
1 tablespoon boiling water

Place egg yolks in a warm bowl. Add salt, mustard, sugar and 1 tablespoon lemon juice. Beat thoroughly. Add half oil, drop by drop, beating thoroughly all the time. When mayonnaise is as thick as stiffly whipped cream, add another tablespoon lemon juice. Still beating, add rest of oil in thin steady stream. Stir in rest of lemon juice and wine vinegar then lastly fold in the boiling water.

BÉCHAMEL SAUCE

1 1/4 cups milk
1 small onion, peeled
1 small carrot, peeled
1/2 small celery stalk
1 blade mace
1 sprig parsley
2 cloves
4 white peppercorns
1 oz. butter
4 tablespoons flour
salt and pepper to taste

Place milk, quartered onion, thickly sliced carrot and thickly sliced celery in a saucepan. Add mace, parsley, cloves and peppercorns. Bring to the boil slowly, stirring. Remove saucepan from heat, cover and leave to stand for about 30 minutes. Strain.
Melt butter in a clean, small, heavy saucepan. Add flour and cook gently, stirring constantly for about 3 minutes. Remove from heat. Gradually add reserved flavoured milk, stirring well after each addition. Cook, stirring with a wooden spoon, until sauce boils and thickens. Simmer for 3-4 minutes. Season with salt and pepper to taste.

SWEDISH SAUCE

1 quantity Basic Mayonnaise (see page 63)
apple purée
1-2 teaspoons grated horseradish

To mayonnaise add an equal quantity apple purée and blend well. Stir in horseradish.

TARTARE SAUCE

1 quantity Basic Mayonnaise (see page 63)
4 tablespoons finely chopped gherkins
2 tablespoons finely chopped capers
1 tablespoon finely chopped parsley

Blend all ingredients together well.

THOUSAND ISLAND SAUCE

1 quantity Basic Mayonnaise (see page 63)
1 hard boiled egg, finely chopped
2 tablespoons chilli sauce
3 tablespoons finely chopped stuffed olives
2 tablespoons finely chopped onion
2 tablespoons finely chopped parsley
2 tablespoons whipped cream, optional

Blend mayonnaise with egg, chilli sauce, olives, onion and parsley. Stir in cream just before serving.
Note: Substitute tomato sauce for chilli sauce if a milder flavour is preferred.

EGG AND LEMON SAUCE

2 eggs
1/2 cup lemon juice
3 tablespoons stock (fish, chicken or beef, according to the dish with which it is to be served)
salt and pepper to taste

Whisk eggs until thick, then gradually beat in the lemon juice. Whisk in the stock. Heat very gently, without boiling, then season to taste. Serve warm.

ANDALOUSE SAUCE

1 quantity Basic Mayonnaise (see page 63)
4 tablespoons tomato paste
4 tablespoons finely chopped pimento
salt and pepper

To Basic Mayonnaise, add tomato paste and pimento,
stir thoroughly. Season to taste.

HORSERADISH SAUCE

1 1/4 cups commercial sour cream
4-6 tablespoons prepared horseradish relish
salt and pepper to taste

Combine all ingredients.

CUCUMBER SAUCE

1 medium sized cucumber
1 1/4 cups Béchamel Sauce (see page 64)
1/4 teaspoon sugar
1/4 teaspoon grated nutmeg
3 tablespoons cream
green food colouring (optional)
salt and pepper to taste

Peel cucumber, slice thickly and remove seeds. Drop into boiling salted water and simmer until tender. Drain thoroughly and chop finely. Combine cucumber, Béchamel Sauce, sugar, nutmeg, cream and reheat gently. Add few drops of green food colouring if desired. Season with salt and pepper to taste. Serve warm or cover and chill before serving.
Note: The Béchamel Sauce may be made using all milk or three-quarters milk, one-quarter cucumber water.

ONION SAUCE

1 large onion
1 1/4 cups Béchamel Sauce (see page 64)
2 tablespoons cream
large pinch of grated nutmeg
salt and pepper

Cut onion into quarters and cook in boiling salted water until tender. Drain and rub through a sieve (or purée in electric blender).
Combine Béchamel Sauce, onion, cream and nutmeg. Reheat gently without boiling. Adjust seasoning to taste, serve warm or chilled.
Note: The Béchamel Sauce may be made using all milk or half milk, half onion water.

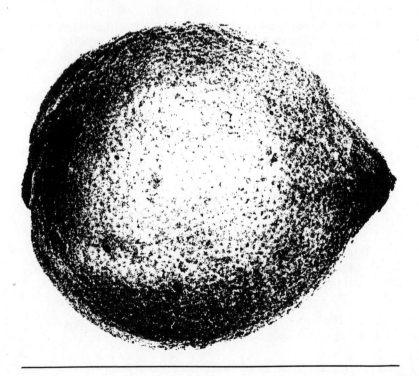

BLACK BEAN SAUCE

4 tablespoons canned black beans
1 clove garlic, crushed
4 shallots
1 tablespoon soy sauce
2 tablespoons sherry
1 teaspoon sugar
1 cup water
3 tablespoons oil
8 oz. minced lean pork
2 tablespoons cornflour
4 tablespoons extra water
2 egg yolks

Wash black beans, drain. Mash beans very well with garlic. Cut shallots into 1/2-inch lengths, mix with soy sauce, sherry, sugar and water. Heat oil, add bean mixture and fry 1-2 minutes. Add pork and continue cooking until browned. Stir in soy sauce mixture, cover and simmer for about 3 minutes. Blend cornflour with extra water, add to pan and cook until thickened. Beat egg yolks lightly and add to pan, stirring. Remove from heat.

CHERRY SAUCE

1 lb. black cherries
2 oz. raisins
5 fl. oz. water
2 tablespoons sugar
pinch of mixed spice

Simmer all ingredients together for about 15 minutes. Press through a sieve and serve warm or cold.

GARLIC SAUCE

1/2 large slice white bread
warm milk
4 cloves garlic, very finely chopped
2 egg yolks
large pinch of salt
1 1/4 cups olive oil
2 teaspoons cold water
juice of 1/2 lemon

Soak bread in milk then squeeze dry. Put in a bowl and, using a wooden spoon, beat to a smooth cream with garlic and egg yolks. Add salt then half the oil, drop by drop, beating thoroughly all the time. As soon as the sauce has thickened, add rest of oil in a thin, steady stream, still beating well. Stir in the water and lemon juice and serve.

CUMBERLAND SAUCE

1/2 teaspoon dry mustard
3 tablespoons brown sugar
large pinch of ground ginger
pinch of cayenne pepper
1/4 teaspoon salt
1 1/4 cups dry red wine
2 cloves
2 tablespoons cornflour
4 tablespoons cold water
1/2 cup red currant jelly
1 teaspoon each finely grated orange and lemon rind
juice of 1 small orange and 1 small lemon

Put mustard, sugar, ginger, cayenne pepper and salt into
a saucepan. Mix to a smooth paste with a little of the wine.
Stir in the rest of the wine. Add cloves, bring to boil,
slowly, stirring. Lower heat and cover pan. Simmer for
10 minutes. Mix cornflour to a smooth paste with cold
water. Add to sauce and stir until thickened. Add all
remaining ingredients and leave over a low heat until
red currant jelly has melted. Adjust seasoning to taste
before serving. Serve warm.

CURRY SAUCE

1 onion
1/2 clove garlic
1 oz. butter or oil
4-6 tablespoons curry powder
1 tablespoon flour
1 1/4 cups stock
1 small apple, grated coarsely
2 oz. desiccated coconut
salt, mustard, lemon juice
1/2 cup cream

Finely chop the onion and garlic. Melt butter or heat oil and immediately add onion and garlic and sprinkle with curry powder and flour. Cook gently but do not allow to brown. Add stock, stir until the sauce becomes smooth and simmer for approximately 20 minutes. Add apple and coconut, salt, mustard and lemon juice to taste. Blend in cream.

SWEET AND SOUR SAUCE

1/2 small red or green capsicum
1 medium sized carrot
1 small bamboo shoot
6 tablespoons vinegar
5 tablespoons sugar
2 tablespoons soy sauce
1/2 teaspoon salt
1 cup chicken stock or water and chicken stock cube
1 teaspoon cornflour
1/2 cup pineapple pieces

Cut capsicum in 1/2-inch squares and carrot into small
wedges. Drop into boiling salted water and cook 5
minutes. Drain. Cut bamboo shoot into thin strips.
Place vinegar and sugar in saucepan, heat, stirring until
sugar is dissolved. Add soy sauce, salt, stock, bamboo
shoot, carrot and capsicum. Simmer 1 minute. Blend
cornflour with a little water, add to pan, bring to boiling
point, stirring and boil for 1-2 minutes. Stir in pineapple
pieces.

MINT SAUCE

1/2 cup white vinegar
2 tablespoons sugar
4 tablespoons finely chopped mint
1/2 cup water

Heat vinegar, add sugar and mint. Cook, stirring for a
few minutes until sugar is dissolved. Add water and cool.

FRESH TOMATO SAUCE

1/4 cup salad oil
1 medium sized onion, very finely chopped
2 oz. bacon, diced
1 clove garlic, finely chopped, optional
1 small carrot, thinly sliced
4 tablespoons flour
12 oz. tomatoes, skinned and chopped
1/4 cup tomato paste
3/4 cup stock or water
1 bay leaf
2 cloves
4 white peppercorns
pinch of basil
1 tablespoon brown sugar
1/2 teaspoon salt
2-inch strip lemon peel
2 teaspoons lemon juice
pepper to taste

Heat oil in large heavy, based saucepan. Add onion,
bacon, garlic (if used) and carrot. Cover pan and fry
gently for about 7 minutes shaking pan frequently. Stir
in flour then tomatoes and tomato paste. Gradually blend
in stock or water. Cook, stirring constantly until sauce
boils and thickens. Add all remaining ingredients and
sauce for 45 minutes, stirring frequently. Strain sauce,
readjust seasoning to taste and serve warm or cold.

QUICK TOMATO SAUCE

1 small onion
1 small apple
1 oz. butter
1 X 5 oz. can tomato paste
2 teaspoons cornflour
1 1/4 cups water
salt and pepper to taste
good pinch of sugar

Peel and grate onion and apple. Heat butter, fry onion for a few minutes, then apple. Add tomato paste and cornflour, blended with water and seasonings. Bring to boil and stir until smooth and thickened. Simmer gently for about 10 minutes, taste, adjust seasonings and add sugar. Serve warm.

PLUM SAUCE

1 cup plum jam
1/2 cup liquid strained from mango chutney
2 tablespoons vinegar
1 1/2 teaspoons sugar

Mix plum jam with mango chutney liquid. Sieve. Heat vinegar, add sugar and stir until dissolved. Combine all ingredients and beat well.
Note: Canned plum sauce can be purchased from some Chinese food stores and can be used instead of the first two ingredients.

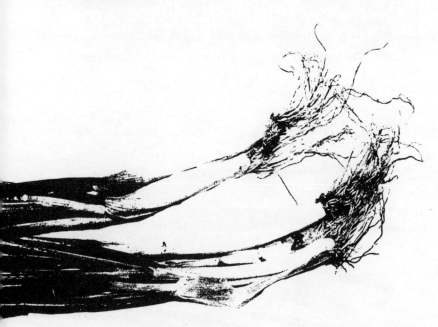

PIQUANT SAUCE

1/2 cup (4 oz.) sugar
1/2 cup white vinegar
pinch of salt
1/4-inch green ginger, crushed
1 cup pineapple juice
1 teaspoon soy sauce
1 teaspoon tomato sauce
1/2 tablespoon cornflour

Place all ingredients except cornflour in saucepan and heat gently, stirring, until boiling. Mix cornflour to a paste with a little water and add. Cook, stirring, for 2 minutes.

RÉMOULADE SAUCE

(Mustard Mayonnaise)

1 1/4 cups olive oil
2 hard-boiled eggs
2 tablespoons wine vinegar
1 egg yolk
1-2 tablespoons mustard

Take the yolks of hard-boiled eggs and cream them with egg yolk and mustard. Add olive oil drop by drop, beating continuously, as for mayonnaise. When all oil has been added stir in vinegar and the finely chopped hard-boiled white of egg.

MUSHROOM SAUCE

4 oz. mushrooms
2 oz. butter
1/2 teaspoon salt
white pepper to taste
2 tablespoons flour
1/2 cup milk
1 tablespoon sherry

Wash mushrooms and cut into thin slices from stem end.
Halve or slice lengthwise. Place in a saucepan, add
butter and seasonings and cook very gently for 10 minutes.
Add flour and milk gradually stirring constantly. Simmer
another 10 minutes, stirring occasionally. Adjust season ing
then add sherry. Serve warm.

OTHER FONDUE RECIPES

A book on fondue cooking would be incomplete without giving the recipes for those fondues which were first mentioned in the introduction—the vegetable preparations, the old original recipe of Brillat-Savarin's and some other recipes for dishes involving the melting of cheese that are also known as fondues. The latter are mainly casseroles which make delicious supper and luncheon dishes. Most can be prepared in advance and kept for a short while in a cool place before being cooked, which can be very useful. Each recipe includes suggestions for serving as these dishes are not served in a fondue pot. Indeed they do not always make a meal in themselves and in some cases, as with the vegetable fondues, they are an ingredient to go into another dish.

BELGIAN PARMESAN FONDUE CAKES

2 1/2 oz. butter
2/3 cup flour
2 1/2 cups milk
salt, pepper and nutmeg to season
5 egg yolks
3/4 cup (3 oz.) grated parmesan cheese
extra flour
egg and fine white breadcrumbs for coating
cayenne pepper, optional

Melt butter in saucepan, add flour and stir over a low
heat for 2-3 minutes, do not allow the roux to brown.
Add milk and bring to the boil, stirring constantly. Season.
Simmer for 25 minutes. Remove from heat and take skin
off top of milk. Mix the egg yolks and cheese together
and stir into milk. Spoon onto a greased plate, spread
a little butter on top and leave to cool.
Press out mixture to 1/2-inch thick on a floured board.
Cut into 1 1/2-inch diameter rounds. Dip each round into
flour then into beaten egg and finally coat in breadcrumbs.
Fry in deep hot oil. Drain and sprinkle lightly with cayenne
pepper if desired.
Serve hot as an hors d'oeuvre or as a savoury.

CHEESE FONDUE BRILLAT-SAVARIN

(translation of the original recipe)
'Weigh the number of eggs which you want to use. This depends on how many people are going to eat with you. Take a piece of good gruyère weighing a third and butter weighing a sixth of the weight of the eggs.
Break the eggs and beat them well in a casserole. Add the butter and the cheese, grated or minced.
Put the casserole on a hot stove and stir with a wooden spoon until the mixture is suitably thickened and is smooth. Add a very little or hardly any salt, depending on the age of the cheese. Add a good portion of pepper, which is one of the distinguishing characteristics of this ancient dish. Serve on a lightly heated dish.'

CAPSICUM FONDUE

1 lb. capsicum
2 tablespoons oil
1 oz. butter
salt and pepper

Skin capsicums by holding under a hot grill, on a fork, until the skin chars and comes away. Remove membranes and seeds and cut into matchstick sized pieces. Heat oil and butter together in a saucepan and cook capsicum gently until softened. Season.
Note: Use in hot and cold sauces, in different kinds of stuffings, with soft eggs, in omelettes, with hot or cold fish, with shellfish, with meat, poultry and vegetables.

BAKED CHICKEN FONDUE

SERVES   4-6
TIME   1 1/4 hours
TEMPERATURE 325-350°F.

1 cup milk
1 cup chicken stock or water and chicken stock
cube
2 oz. butter
2 cups diced cooked chicken
1 1/2 cups breadcrumbs
1/2 cup (2 oz.) grated parmesan cheese
salt and pepper to taste
1/4 teaspoon mustard
1 teaspoon tarragon
juice of 1/2 lemon
4 eggs, separated

Heat milk, stock and butter in a saucepan until butter
is melted. Stir in chicken, breadcrumbs, cheese,
seasonings, lemon juice and tarragon. Beat egg yolks
lightly and add, stirring until mixture thickens. Do not
allow to boil. Remove from heat. Whisk egg whites until
stiff and fold into mixture. Pour into a greased casserole.
Stand casserole in a shallow dish of hot water (water should
come halfway up the sides of the casserole). Bake in a
moderately slow oven for 1 1/4 hours or until golden.
Serve as a luncheon or supper dish with a green salad.
Note: Other poultry may be substituted for the chicken.

BAKED CIDER FONDUE

SERVES   4-6
TIME   1 1/4 hours
TEMPERATURE   325-350°F.

1 cup milk
1 small onion, chopped
1 cup cider
1/2 cup grated apple
salt and dry mustard to taste
3 cups (12 oz.) grated cheddar cheese
2 1/2 cups diced white bread
4 eggs, separated
2 oz. butter
2 teaspoons cinnamon

Place milk and onion in a saucepan. Scald. Add the cider, apple, seasonings, cheese and 2 cups diced bread. Stir until cheese has melted. Beat egg yolks and add. Whisk egg whites until stiff and fold into mixture. Pour into a greased casserole, dot with butter and sprinkle with cinnamon and remaining bread cubes. Bake in a moderately slow oven for 1 1/4 hours or until golden brown.
Serve as a luncheon or supper dish with a salad.

VEGETABLE FONDUE

2 carrots
1 small turnip
1 leek
1 onion
2 stalks celery
salt
1 teaspoon castor sugar
2 oz. butter
1/2 cup chicken stock or water and chicken stock cube

Chop vegetables finely and place in a heavy saucepan.
Add salt and sugar then butter, cut into small pieces.
Stir over a low heat until butter is melted and the
vegetables are golden brown. Add stock and cook very
slowly stirring occasionally until nearly all the liquid has
evaporated.
Use this fondue as a garnish for grills or as a base for
sauces or stuffings.

BAKED ONION FONDUE

SERVES   4-6
TIME   40 minutes
TEMPERATURE   350-375 °F.

6 slices of bread
butter
1 1/2 cups (6 oz.) coarsely grated cheddar cheese
3 eggs
3 cups milk
salt and pepper to taste
1 large onion, chopped

Trim crusts off bread and butter each slice liberally.
Cut bread into 1-inch squares and place in a buttered
casserole. Sprinkle the cheese evenly on the bread. Beat
together the eggs, milk, seasonings and onion and pour
over cheese. Bake in a moderate oven for 40 minutes or
until set and golden brown.
Serve as a luncheon or supper dish with a green salad.

TOMATO FONDUE SAUCE

1 tablespoon oil
1/2 oz. butter
1 onion, chopped
6 tomatoes, skinned, seeded and roughly chopped
salt and pepper
1 clove garlic, crushed
1 tablespoon chopped parsley

Heat oil and butter together in a saucepan. Fry onion
gently until beginning to brown. Add tomatoes, salt,
pepper and garlic. Cook very gently until the liquid has
almost disappeared. Add parsley. Use as desired.
Note: Tomato Fondue Sauce is used for an infinite
number of dishes mainly for those called à la provençale,
à la portugaise, or à la madrilène. It is a garnish for eggs
and for vegetables such as mushrooms, zucchinis,
eggplant, artichoke hearts, etc. When made with all oil
(2 tablespoons oil—no butter), and chilled, tomato fondue
sauce is often used in the preparation of cold hors
d'oeuvre.

MORE TABLE-TOP COOKING

To divert a little from fondue making. The following recipes are for other forms of cooking at the table. You may have been very impressed with food being cooked at your table in a restaurant and if you follow the recipes in this chapter you will see just how easy it is to prepare and serve these dishes.

The first essential is a spirit burner which looks attractive on the table, and is easily regulated.

Secondly one needs a pan in which to cook the food. The type of pan will vary according to the food to be cooked, it can be a chafing dish, flambée pan, omelette and crêpe pan, frying pan or a specially designed wine bowl, for the preparation of hot drinks. A chafing dish is normally accompanied by a water bath and can be used with or without it. Often the food is cooked over a direct flame and then the water bath is used to keep the completed dish hot without it becoming dry or over cooked. A flambée pan can be a specially made pan but an ordinary frying pan will suffice if one is not available. An omelette pan should not be the same pan as used for frying, it should be a small heavy pan which is used exclusively for making omelettes and crepês. A wine bowl can be used for making many delicious hot drinks. It should be deep, and large enough to serve at least 10 people. A sugar holder is a useful addition and is a big part of the preparing and serving of some drinks. A sugar loaf (or cubes if a loaf is not available) is placed on the holder over the drink, spirits poured over and ignited. Turn out the lights and watch the flames flickering!

The third and last thing one needs, for really impressive entertaining in this fashion, is a co-operative man. Husbands can be trained to use a flambée pan or chafing dish expertly which not only helps to take some of the burden of cooking away from the hostess but many men like to impress and really enjoy being the centre of attraction at dinner parties!!

Two more traditionally Swiss dishes.
Serve them for luncheon or supper.

SWISS BREAD 'ROSTI'

SERVES 4

8 oz. Swiss cheese
14 oz. stale white bread
3/4 cup milk
3/4 cup water
4 oz. butter
1 onion, finely grated
pepper

Cut cheese and bread into thin slices and put in a bowl.
Heat milk and water together until scalding hot, but not
boiling, and pour over cheese and bread. Allow to stand
for about 30 minutes. Melt butter in frying pan, sauté
onion until soft, add cheese and bread (which
should have soaked up all the liquid by now) and fry on
a low heat, turning continually until golden brown. Dust
with a little pepper before serving.

SWISS CHEESE PANCAKES

SERVES 4-6

2 cups (8 oz.) flour
3/4 cup milk
3/4 cup water
4 eggs
1 teaspoon salt
3 oz. butter
1 1/4 cups (6 oz.) grated Swiss cheese

Sieve flour into a bowl, make a well in centre. Beat
together milk, water, eggs and salt and add to flour,
pouring into the well in centre of flour. Gradually stir
in the flour around the edge until all is combined. Beat
well. Allow batter to stand for 30 minutes. Add cheese.
Melt a little butter in frying pan, add enough batter to
cover base of pan, cook until golden brown, turning once.
Roll up and serve at once with Quick Tomato Sauce
(see recipe page 76).

Main course dishes for extra special dinners, they are useful if time is short and you want to serve a meal to be remembered.

BEEF STROGANOFF

SERVES 4

1 1/2 lb. fillet steak
2 1/2 oz. butter
2 shallots, finely chopped
salt, pepper and paprika pepper
1/2 cup sour cream

Cut meat into pieces 2-inches long and 1/4-inch wide. Melt 1/2 oz. butter in chafing dish over direct flame and fry shallots until tender. Remove. Heat 2 oz. butter, add steak and sauté for 3-5 minutes until cooked. Season with salt, pepper and paprika pepper. Add shallots to meat and stir in sour cream. Reheat without boiling, adjust seasonings. Serve at once with hot buttered noodles.

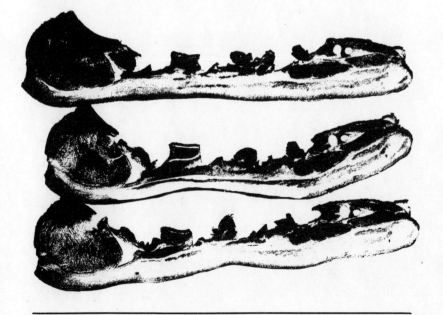

GREEN PEPPER KEBABS

SERVES 6

1 lb. beef fillet
12 rashers bacon
2 green peppers
6 oz. butter, melted
fresh white breadcrumbs
salt and pepper

Cut meat into 3/4-inch cubes. Cut bacon and de-seeded green peppers into 3/4-inch squares.
Alternate meat, bacon and peppers on 6 small skewers, brush with melted butter and roll in breadcrumbs. Season well. Heat remaining butter in chafing dish over flame and fry kebabs gently, turning when necessary, until cooked. Served with hot boiled rice and Tossed Green Salad (see recipe page 53).

SPAGHETTI MARINARA

SERVES 6

8 oz. fish fillets (flounder, sole or John Dory)
1 lb. cooked prawns
2 cloves garlic, crushed
oil
1 lb. tomatoes, skinned and chopped
salt and pepper
1/2 level teaspoon sugar
1/2 cup dry white wine
1 teaspoon oregano
1 lb. spaghetti
chopped parsley

Skin fish fillets, cut into bite sized pieces, shell prawns.
Fry garlic, in chafing dish over direct flame, in a little
hot oil until softened, add fish fillets, cook until lightly
tinted, drain. Pour off any oil left in pan, add tomatoes,
salt, pepper and sugar. Cook rapidly about 15 minutes,
stir in wine, oregano, fish fillets and prawns. Simmer until
fish and prawns are heated through. Serve with hot
buttered spaghetti and garnish with chopped parsley.

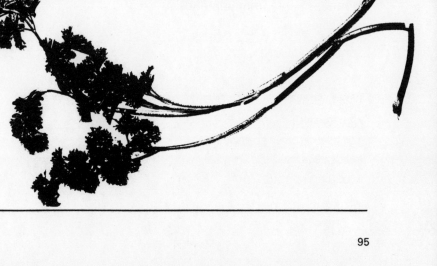

PAELLA

SERVES 4

1/4 cup olive oil
4 cooked chicken pieces
(legs or wings)
1 onion, chopped
1 clove garlic, crushed
5 cups chicken stock
2 medium sized tomatoes, skinned and chopped
4 oz. rice
pinch of saffron
1 small crayfish
4 king prawns
8 mussels
8 oz. cooked peas
1 red pepper, diced

Heat oil in chafing dish or large frying pan over direct flame, fry chicken, onion and garlic until chicken is browned all over. Add half stock, simmer 15 minutes. Add tomatoes, rice and rest of stock. Simmer 5 minutes, stir in saffron. Arrange the crayfish pieces, prawns, mussels, peas and pepper attractively in pan. Cook until rice is tender and has absorbed most of the liquid, 15-20 minutes. Serve immediately.

Fondue dishes shown on the following four colour pages are (in order):

KRAMBAMBULI

BOURGUIGNONNE FONDUE

PEACHES FLAMBÉE

BLUSHING FONDUE

VEAL PICCATE

SERVES 4

4 x 4 oz. thin veal steaks
lemon juice
salt and pepper
flour
1 oz. butter
2 tablespoons oil
1/2 cup marsala
1/4 cup chicken stock
lemon wedges for garnish
green noodles for serving

Place veal steaks between two pieces of plastic and pound until very thin, about 1/8-inch thick. Sprinkle with lemon juice, leave for 10 minutes. Season with salt and pepper and coat lightly in flour. Melt butter in chafing dish over direct flame, add oil. When very hot, add veal steaks and cook quickly until golden brown on both sides, turning once. Stir in marsala and stock. Simmer 2 minutes. Serve veal on a heated platter and pour sauce over, garnish with lemon wedges. Serve with hot buttered green noodles.

SUKIYAKI

SERVES 4

4 oz. mushrooms
4 oz. bamboo shoots
1 large onion
2 shallots
2 leeks
2 sticks celery
1 lb. French beans or spinach
2 oz. bean curd
1 lb. fillet steak
2 tablespoons sugar
4 tablespoons soy sauce
salt and pepper
hot boiled rice for serving
1/4 cup oil
4 eggs, optional

Simmer mushrooms in 1/2 cup water for 2 minutes.
Drain, reserve liquor. Slice mushrooms, bamboo shoots
and onion very finely. Chop shallots, leeks and celery,
slice beans or spinach and bean curd. Cut the meat into
wafer thin slices. Arrange all these ingredients in neat
piles on plates. Make sauce by combining reserved
mushroom liquor, sugar, soy sauce and seasonings. Put
rice into a dish to keep hot.
Bring all Sukiyaki ingredients to the table. Heat oil in
large chafing dish over direct flame, put in ingredients,
adding sauce gradually. Cook for 10-15 minutes. Serve
on hot rice on individual plates. Top each plate with a
raw egg, if desired.

CHICKEN FLAMBÉ

SERVES 4

1 x 2 1/2 lb. chicken
3 oz. butter
salt and pepper
3 tablespoons calvados or brandy
3/4 cup cream
2 egg yolks

Cut chicken into quarters. Put 2 oz. butter in flambée pan
and brown chicken all over. Season, lower heat and
cook gently for 30 minutes or until tender. Pour over the
calvados, ignite. When flames subside, remove chicken,
add cream and egg yolks and reheat. Do not allow to boil.
Stir, scraping bottom of pan and add rest of butter bit
by bit. Adjust seasoning, pour over chicken pieces. Serve
with hot boiled rice.
Note: Chicken may be pre-cooked and just heated
through in butter in the flambée pan.

HERBED VEAL KIDNEYS FLAMBÉS

SERVES 4

4 small veal kidneys
5 oz. butter
4 tablespoons fresh herbs
juice of 1 lemon
1/2 cup cognac
salt and pepper

Trim kidneys, remove all skin and hard fat. Cut into thin slices. Heat 1 1/2 oz. butter and when very hot sear slices on both sides. Drain, place on a heated dish.
Heat remaining butter in chafing dish, add herbs, lemon juice and kidneys. Pour over cognac, ignite. When flames subside, season to taste and serve.

TASMANIAN SCALLOPS FLAMBÉES

SERVES 4

1 1/4 cups white wine
12 scallops
8 oz. mushrooms
4 oz. butter
3 tablespoons cognac
1/2 cup cream
salt and pepper

Heat wine, add scallops and simmer until scallops are
tender. Wash and slice mushrooms.
Ten minutes before serving, melt butter in flambée pan
and sauté mushrooms until tender. Add prepared, drained
scallops. Cook 5-6 minutes. Add cognac, ignite. When
flames have subsided, stir in cream, reheat and season
to taste. Serve with hot boiled rice.

Quick, delicious and very easy to cook, these desserts will delight your guests.

BANANAS FLAMBÉS

SERVES 6

1 cup sweet red wine
1/2 cup brown sugar
1 teaspoon orange rind, grated
1/2 teaspoon each ground nutmeg and cinnamon
1/4 teaspoon ground cloves
6 bananas
juice of 1 lemon
chopped almonds
4 tablespoons rum
cream or ice cream, for serving

Put wine, sugar, orange rind and spices into flambée pan. Heat gently, stirring until sugar is melted. Peel bananas, sprinkle well with lemon juice. Place in syrup and poach gently until soft and tender. Sprinkle with almonds, pour rum over, ignite and serve with cream or ice cream.

CRÊPES SUZETTE

SERVES 4

Crêpes:
1 cup (4 oz.) plain flour
pinch of salt
2 eggs
1 cup milk
1/4 cup water
butter

red currant jelly or orange Filling (see below)
brandy, curaçao or grand marnier

Sieve flour and salt together. Gradually beat in eggs, milk and water until batter is very smooth. Heat a little butter in crêpe pan, cover base of pan with a very thin layer of batter and cook quickly until brown and crisp, turning once. Fill each crêpe with red currant jelly or orange mixture, fold in four. Remove from pan and keep warm. When all the batter is used up, return filled crêpes all together to pan, pour over a little brandy or curaçao and ignite. When flames subside, serve at once.

Orange Filling:
2 oz. butter
1/4 cup (2 oz.) castor sugar
juice and grated rind of 1 orange

Cream butter and sugar, beat in orange juice and rind.

CHESTNUT CRÊPES

SERVES 4

12 prepared crêpes (see recipe
for Crêpes Suzette, page 103)
canned chestnut purée
apricot jam, melted
2 tablespoons cointreau
1/2 cup slivered almonds, toasted

Spread each crêpes with chestnut purée and roll up
tightly. Place in chafing dish, brush with apricot jam.
Pour over warmed cointreau, ignite. When flames have
subsided, sprinkle with almonds and serve.

SIMPLE FRUIT FLAMBÉES

bananas, apricots or plums
water
butter
sugar
brandy

Halve the fruit, put into flambée pan with little butter,
sugar and water. Heat gently until fruit is soft but unbroken
and has absorbed the liquid. Pour a little brandy over
fruit, allow to warm, ignite and serve immediately.
Note: The amounts of water, butter and sugar used in
this recipe vary so considerably that it would be better if
you start with very little of each and add more if necessary
during the cooking time.

GLAZED PINEAPPLE SLICES

SERVES 4

1 can (16 oz.) pineapple slices
2 oz. butter
1/4 cup brown sugar
1 tablespoon rum
whipped cream for serving

Drain pineapple slices. Melt butter in chafing dish,
add pineapple slices and heat through. Sprinkle with
brown sugar and then rum, ignite. Serve, when flames
have subsided, with whipped cream.

PEACHES FLAMBÉES

SERVES 4

8 canned peach halves
1/2 cup brandy
1/2 cup reserved peach syrup
grated rind of 1 orange
1/3 cup red currant jelly
vanilla ice cream and flaked almonds for serving

Drain peach halves well, reserve 1/2 cup syrup, pour half
brandy over peaches and allow to marinate 1 hour. Heat
reserved peach syrup with orange rind in chafing dish over
direct flame, reduce liquid by half. Add jelly and stir
until melted. Add peaches to chafing dish, heat. Pour
remaining brandy over peaches, ignite. When flames
subside serve with vanilla ice cream and sprinkle the
almonds over the top.

RUM OMELETTE

SERVES 2

4 eggs
salt
2 oz. butter
extra butter, melted
icing sugar

Beat eggs and salt together very well. Heat butter in
omelette pan until bubbling and hot. Pour eggs into pan
and stir gently with a fork bringing the cooking egg
on the outside of pan, into the centre. When omelette
is cooked but still creamy, roll up. Brush top of omelette
with a little melted butter, sprinkle with icing sugar and
pour over a little warmed rum. Ignite rum and serve
flaming.

BRANDIED APPLES

SERVES 3-4

2 oz. butter
2 apples, cored and sliced but not peeled
2 teaspoons icing sugar
2 tablespoons chopped walnuts
1 cup cream
1 tablespoon brandy

Heat butter in chafing dish over direct flame. Saute apple rings gently until tender. Sprinkle with icing sugar and nuts. Whip cream, add brandy. Serve apples in individual dishes, topped with brandied cream.

These recipes for deliciously different drinks will be welcomed by every hostess. They are guaranteed to warm your guests in winter and are especially good for apres-ski parties.

GLOEGG

SERVES 10-12

5 cups brandy
1-2 cinnamon sticks
5 cardamom pods
peel of 1 orange, blanched
4 cloves
4 oz. raisins
4 oz. almonds
1 sugar loaf or 10 oz. sugar cubes

Place all ingredients, except sugar, into wine bowl.
Allow to stand for a few hours. Place sugar loaf or cubes in sugar holder across wine bowl. Ladle some of the brandy mixture over the sugar and ignite. When all sugar has melted cover with lid to put out flames. Stir, and serve in heatproof glasses.
Variations: For a slightly different flavour add 2 finely chopped figs and 1/2-inch green ginger to brandy. Add 2 1/2 cups dry red wine or 3/4 cup madeira to Gloegg just before serving.

KRAMBAMBULI

SERVES 10-12

2 x 26 oz. bottles light, dry red wine
juice of 2 oranges
juice of 1 lemon
2 1/2 cups rum
1 sugar loaf or 10 oz. sugar cubes

Pour wine into wine bowl and heat on burner. Do not
allow to boil. Add orange and lemon juice. Place the
sugar holder across the bowl and add sugar loaf or cubes.
Warm rum and soak the sugar, ignite. When flames start
to subside, add more rum. The sugar should be melted
with the last drop of rum. Stir, and serve in heatproof
glasses.

GLUEWEIN

SERVES 10-15

10 cups claret
juice of 3 lemons
2 cinnamon sticks
1/2 teaspoon ground cloves
1/2 teaspoon ground nutmeg
3/4-1 cup (5-6 oz.) brown sugar
2 lemons, sliced
4 cups lemonade, optional

Mix all ingredients together in wine bowl and heat gently.
Serve very hot, not boiling. Add lemonade, if used, and
reheat just before serving.
Variation: Substitute orange juice and sliced oranges
for lemons if desired.

MULLED ALE

5 cups ale
1/2 cup rum or brandy
2 tablespoons sugar
pinch of ground cloves
pinch of ground ginger

Mix all ingredients together in wine bowl. Heat gently,
do not boil. Serve in heatproof glasses.

MULLED CIDER

SERVES 10-12

5 cups sweet cider
3 cloves
2-inch stick cinnamon
3 whole allspice
2 oz. brown sugar
2 red apples and grated nutmeg for decoration

Put cider, cloves, cinnamon, allspice and sugar into wine
bowl. Heat until boiling, simmer for 15 minutes. Allow
to stand 12 hours, strain and reheat. Decorate with apples,
cored and sliced, and nutmeg. Serve in heatproof glasses.

To complete the perfect dinner. . . .

IRISH COFFEE

SERVES 1

1 tablespoon Irish whisky
1/2 cup strong black coffee
sugar to taste
cream, lightly whipped

Warm Irish coffee glass, add whisky and, if liked, ignite.
Add coffee and sugar to taste, stir well. Hold a spoon
upside down over the glass and pour cream carefully
over so that it floats on top of the coffee and does not
mix in. Do not stir. The coffee is drunk through the cream.

ACKNOWLEDGEMENTS

The editor would like to thank the following for their assistance in providing information, equipment and photographs for Fondue Cookery.

Switzerland Cheese Association,
New York, U.S.A.
Spring Brothers, Metalware Manufacturers,
Eschlikan, Switzerland
Incorporated Agencies Pty. Ltd.,
Sydney, Australia
Century Imports, Canberra, Australia

All questions relating to the fondue equipment shown in this book can be referred to the suppliers, Dexam International Limited, Haslemere, Surrey. (Applies to the UK only.)

INDEX